Little Baba

Hakeem Khan

BookLeaf Publishing

Presentation by *BookLeaf Publishing*

Web: www.bookleafpub.com

E-mail: info@bookleafpub.com

ISBN: 9789357210065

First edition 2022

DEDICATION

In honour of my beloved baby boy, Hakeem.

ACKNOWLEDGEMENT

I would like to thank Book Leaf Publishing for giving me the opportunity and platform to share my work.
I would also like to thank the staff at the Labour Ward at Stepping Hill Hospital for looking after me with compassion and care during a very difficult time in my life.

Baby

I yearn to see your face
I yearn to feel your touch
Though we've never met
I love you very much

I can only wonder how you are
I can only guess if you're well
I hope you're strong little one
Only time will tell

We've waited for so long
To meet you dear child
Tell me how is it
I still continue to smile

Stay strong and grow my little one
Mummy would like to meet you soon
I hope you're ready for all the fun
I can't wait until you're due

Flowers

A bouquet of flowers where your basket should be
A hole inside my heart
Emptiness ripens in my stomach today
Longing for you since your depart

Grief where laughter should be
Silence in the house
No words can fill the void I must say,
All hope to be renounced

Emptiness where joy should be
Little clothes that were never worn
Tears shedding with no control
The love we felt since you were born

A heavy chest where my child should lay
Breathe through another day
A loss we cannot replace but,
So many flowers were delivered today

Oh my dear child

Oh my dear child

My heart is hurting without your love
My house is empty without your presence
My stomach growls without intent
My arms reach for your essence

Oh my dear child

You left my house in silence
You left my heart in pain
My heart aches without you
My tears shed like rain

Oh my dear child

The life I imagined with your love
To give you the best, I always cared
If only you were close to me
The moments we could have shared

Oh my dear child

It's cold without your cuddles
I'm lost without your love

I just hope you're safe and happy
Warm in heaven above

Wake up another day

Your absence fills the silence
As I wake up and face another day.
Tears from the sky comfort my heart
Whilst another day passes away.

Grief fills the rooms as the walls sigh
A hole only you can fill,
The clouds swiftly float away
Only my heart is standing still.

Life moves on and time passes
But no, Time doesn't heal.
As the world gets on with the day in front
Only a mother knows what she feels

I woke up another day
My beloved son never did wake,
My heart crippled as I walk the Earth
Nothing comforts the gut wrenching ache

Long to...

How I long to hold you in my arms
How I wish to cuddle you and keep you warm

If only words could convey my feelings
I'd write to you and begin my healing

How I long to kiss your lovely cheeks
And feel your love, I wish to seek

A future mapped out with your presence
And now a life lived, in your absence

How I long to see your lovely face
No harm done, without a trace

I'd hold you tight and never let go
I'd snuggle up and let time go slow

How I long to hold you in my arms
How I wish to cuddle you and keep you warm

How deep is your cut

Spit words out like spitting itself
No idea how deep they go,
If my side works then let it be
Don't tell me to reap what i sow.

Drop all bombshells drop them fast
It's only words after all,
No idea how deep you've cut
Emotional turmoils build a wall.

Stand tall and speak your mind
Be proud; They teach today..
Smart is witty, smart is critical
Survival of the fittest, as they say..

Spit venom or spit fragrance
Beholders' eye you can't transform,
How deep the cut is, you can't see
Beholder keeps his calm

Age

Age is but a number
Life isn't measured in years
We're all counting the inevitable orbit
What is it mankind fears

It's moments that divide our lives
Time stops when hearts skip a beat,
Yet it's the beats we're counting
Who is it we're trying to cheat

Youth is celebrated without achievement
Is capturing innocence our plan?
Has age old wisdom lost its importance
Or has humanity reached its span

Age has become the enemy
The enemy within us all
Isn't time a healer,
Don't we need time to enthrall

My dear

Sharpen your tongue my dear
Sharp as they come
Fast as they fall my dear
Before your mouth becomes numb

Razor like teeth my dear
Piercing through ears that are sore
Rapid and jagged my dear
With words they tore

Sharpen your tongue my dear
It's the way forward in life
Faster the better my dear
Always stick in the knife

Life is tough my dear
Sharpen the edges of your tongue
Learn the words my dear
Learn the words to the sharpest song

Monsters

I wish all the monsters would go away
I wish I could teach them how to play

Pack it all up at the end of the day
Teach them to put their toys away

The world is full of ghouls and ghosts
So why do I meet the monsters most

I'd like to know how monsters feel
Late at night when the masks have peeled

I'm surrounded by hatred from their wrath
I wish I could find another path

I wish all the monsters would go away
I wish they'd stop forcing me to play

Little Baba

A tiny face and a tiny body
All wrapped up, my bundle of joy
The moment I waited for, bittersweet
Born asleep, my beloved baby boy

Many months and hours of labour
The moment was finally here
At last a child, we're a family now
Let's hold back that tear

But we have to say goodbye
Because he's already gone
But we've bought so many things
None of which he's worn

And now my heart is torn

You have to let me mourn

Why is it me that has to accept
They buried his body as i sat here and wept
I cried out my heart as they continued their day
Not knowing how long this pain came to stay

No more dreams and no more wonder

All that's left is rain and thunder
Nobody understands the hole in my heart
I loved him dearly right from the start

One day little Baba, we will meet again
A garden with no thunder or rain
That day you'll pull me by the cord
A promise to us, from our dear Lord

Until that day I will have to keep strong
Until you're in my arms, where you belong
Rotating shifts, the Sun and the Moon
My little Baba, gone too soon

Pain

Months of love and joy I spent
Wondering, how the time went
Waiting eagerly to see your face
To snuggle up in a warm embrace

Labouring, the hours past by
Excruciating pain only mothers survive
A moment of peace we came to meet
What should have been relief, after all the heat

They say the pain goes when the baby cries
But my son didn't open his eyes
Silence prevailed in the empty room
Realisation, of the impending doom

Your child is heaven dear
No need to worry nor shed a tear
Peaceful, Painless he may be
But what about me?

I'm happy he's in heaven as such
But why does this hurt so much
Words of comfort only stay a while
Wear my shoes, and walk a mile

To all the mothers who bled out
Buried their children and left without
Clutching your heart and passing through
I know your pain, I feel it too

One day

One day my son we will meet again
A place with no harm nor pain

A garden with fruits only we can imagine
A place none can harm, nor lessen

A reward for the hardship we had to endure
A place where love remains so pure

One day my child you will pull me to you
That day you will get, love that's overdue

One day Baba you can tell me the story
Of your days passed in heaven in effortless glory

The heaven where your soul resides
A place where all nature abides

The heaven where the best ones go
You were chosen to blossom and grow

One day my son we will be together
In the garden God promised, peacefully forever

Moment

A moment in my arms
But a lifetime in my heart,
A brief chance to love
But I loved you from the start

Tiny footprints left me heartbroken
A moment I cannot forget,
For a mother is a lifetime
From the moment a child is beget

Gone but not forgotten
My beloved baby boy,
We long to meet again my son
With happiness and joy

Mother's day comes and goes
Only the empty arms feel bare,
Difficult smiles during difficult days
Like a suit of armour we wear

I long for the blissful moment
In heaven we shall meet,
That moment that shall span to eternity
When pain can no longer defeat

Alone ●

If love alone could keep you here
You'd never leave my side,
Loneliness is now my comfort
Ever since the day you died

Alone in the deepest depths of grief
I grasp at those little memories,
If love alone could keep you with me
Loneliness couldn't seize the opportunities

I didn't think it's possible to cry so much
If only my tears could bring you back,
My heart would be filled with so much love
No heartbreak, not even a crack

Grief lasts longer than sympathy
That's why we're so alone,
Clutching at your memories
Loneliness sets the tone

Would you know I'm a mother ❤

A postpartum belly, stretch marks run wild
At least my body, acknowledges my child
Arms that are empty, heart's in pain
Would you know I'm a mother, I can pertain

A life so different to what I'd planned
No toys no joys in my hand,
Daily tasks without disruption
What I'd give, for your interruption

Visits to your grave is my daily walk
Noise in the background, I never heard you talk
Flowers by your side set down by your mother
A love so pure unlike any other

Walking through the park watching the view
A life so lonely I never knew,
Up all night remembering your face
How I wish you were here, in my embrace

Today

Today's the day I should've brought you home
Instead I'm sat here all alone

I'm sat here remembering how I held you once
Only to be taken from me, after a glance

I love you more than words can say
Words don't have enough, depth to convey

If life could prepare me for this pain
I'd never set foot on Earth again

I've loved you since I knew you were mine
If my love could save you, we'd be fine

Today's the day my baby was due
Instead he went and skipped the queue

He came too early and left too soon
Breaking my heart and leaving an empty womb

Overwhelming emotions, if today could wait
I wouldn't have to call it, my baby's due date

Storm

I'm sorry there's no heartbeat

Split second and everything changed
My life became upside down
In one moment I lost my son
Tears and sorrow until I drowned

Lost all my hopes and all my dreams
Left with empty arms
Silence wailed in the empty room
A grieved mother sat so calm

A storm inside the calmed parent
A storm waiting to destroy
Every inch of happiness
Every hope, dream and joy

Waves of severe pain
A storm that chose to dare
Emotional turmoil
Leaving inhabitants in despair

Breathing Earthside whilst my son isn't here
Everything changed in my life
A gut wrenching ache that couldn't be explained

As if I'd been struck with a knife

Days are endless, the nights are longer
Dates that should have been filled with fun
A storm that drowns the strongest,
Whilst patiently awaiting the sun

Time

They say time heals
And everything runs its course,
But the loss of a child
Is a pain that never loses force

You're never quite the same
Nor does the pain ever end,
Forever grieving silently
Smiling and having to pretend

Moving forward and moving on
Is all the advice you ever hear,
Are you uncomfortable listening to my story
And watching me shed a tear

Dont worry parent you'll have another
Time will heal your pain,
What cruel remarks you have to hear
Time and time again

Time is healer
But do we really heal?
Or do bereaved parents behave well
And hide, how we feel

Life without you 💔

I dreamt of meeting you for so long
Now that hope is no longer there
You were such a wanted child
I'm devastated beyond despair

It's hard to believe I have to continue to live
The rest of my life without you,
I imagined a world with you in my arms
Now I don't like the future view

Memories missed and cheeks not kissed
How can I choose to move on?
Arms that are bare and hope no longer there
Everything is a reminder you've gone

I'm not afraid of death anymore
I'm afraid to live.
Knowing you're not here everyday
All this love, I cannot give

STOP

Stop telling me how to grieve
Dont tell me how to carry the pain
Stop expecting me to run along
No! I can't dance in the rain

This isn't just 'one of those things'
It's heavier than you think
A loss that is irreplaceable
Sometimes I'm worried, I might just sink...

Were you pregnant for all those months
Did you give birth to a child
Did you then say goodbye to him
And watch the world move on and smile

You never get over the loss of a child
You don't know how much I've lost
No one knows the magnitude of pain
Alone, I know the emotional cost

The memories I will never have
The time I never spent
I didn't just lose a baby
That day, my whole life went

Stop telling me how to grieve
My heart already carries so much sorrow
Too many times we pretend we're ok
The smiles and laughs we borrow

I'm sick of minimising my grief
I'm tired of having to live
To make others feel comfortable,
I don't have much more to give

Everybody just wants to hear you're fine
Is it too sad for you to bear?
Guess what, I have to live every minute like this
Stop advising and be aware

Dear Daddy ❤

I call you Babba every day
Skipping in heaven as i play

I know you miss me very much
After a final glance and a final touch

I know it hurt when you said goodbye
I know you remember me and you cry

I know your heart breaks when you think of me
I'm in a better place, one day you'll see

I know you wish to hold me tight
Dont worry daddy I'm safe, day and night

We'll be reunited in happiness and joy
A message to you, from your beloved baby boy